Fragments of Xenophanes

by Xenophanes, translated by John Burnet

TABLE OF CONTENTS

Fragments of Xenophanes

Fragments according to the text and arrangement of Diels.

Fragment 1

Now is the floor clean, and the hands and cups of all; one sets twisted garlands on our heads, another hands us fragrant ointment on a salver. The mixing bowl stands ready, full of gladness, and there is more wine at hand that promises never to leave us in the lurch, soft and smelling of flowers in the jars. In the midst the frankincense sends up its holy scent, and there is cold water, sweet and clean. Brown loaves are set before us and a lordly table laden with cheese and rich honey. The altar in the midst is clustered round with flowers; song and revel fill the halls.

But first it is meet that men should hymn the god with joy, with holy tales and pure words; then after libation and prayer made that we may have strength to do right—for that is in truth the first thing to do—no sin is it to drink as much as a man can take and get home without an attendant, so he be not stricken in years. And of all men is he to be praised who after drinking gives goodly proof of himself in the trial of skill,[1] as memory and strength will serve him. Let him not sing of Titans and Giants—those fictions of the men of old—nor of turbulent civil broils in which is no good thing at all; but to give heedful reverence to the gods is ever good.

Fragment 2

What if a man win victory in swiftness of foot, or in the pentathlon, at Olympia, where is the precinct of Zeus by Pisa's springs, or in wrestling, – what if by cruel boxing or that fearful sport men call pankration he become more glorious in the citizens' eyes, and win a place of honour in the sight of all at the games, his food at the public cost from the State, and a gift to be an heirloom for him, – what if he conquer in the chariot-race, – he will not deserve all this for his portion so much as I do. Far better is our art than the strength of men and of horses! These are but thoughtless judgements, nor is it fitting to set strength before goodly art.[2] Even if there arise a mighty boxer among a people, or one great in the pentathlon or at wrestling, or one excelling in swiftness of foot—and that stands in honour before all tasks of men at the games—the city would be none the better governed for that. It is but little joy a city gets of it if a man conquer at the games by Pisa's banks; it is not this that makes fat the store-houses of a city.

Fragment 3

They learnt dainty and unprofitable ways from the Lydians, so long as they were free from hateful tyranny; they went to the market-place with cloaks of purple dye, not less than a thousand of them all told, vainglorious and proud of their comely tresses, reeking with fragrance from cunning salves.

Fragment 4

Nor would a man mix wine in a cup by pouring out the wine first, but water first and wine on the top of it.

Fragment 5

Thou didst send the thigh-bone of a kid and get for it the fat leg of a fatted bull, a worthy guerdon for a man to get, whose glory is to reach every part of Hellas and never to pass away, so long as Greek songs last.[3]

Fragment 7

And now I will turn to another tale and point the way . . .
. Once they say that he (Pythagoras) was passing by when
a dog was being beaten and spoke this word: "Stop! don't
beat it! For it is the soul of a friend that I recognised when
I heard its voice."[4]

Fragment 8

There are by this time threescore years and seven that have tossed my careworn soul[5] up and down the land of Hellas; and there were then five-and-twenty years from my birth, if I can say aught truly about these matters.

Fragment 9

Much weaker than an aged man.

Fragment 10

Since all at first have learnt according to Homer . . . .

Fragment 11

Homer and Hesiod have ascribed to the gods all things that are a shame and a disgrace among mortals, stealings and adulteries and deceivings of one another.

Fragment 12

Since they have uttered many lawless deeds of the gods, stealings and adulteries and deceivings of one another.

Fragment 14

But mortals deem that the gods are begotten as they are,
and have clothes like theirs, and voice and form.

Fragment 15

Yes, and if oxen and horses or lions had hands, and could paint with their hands, and produce works of art as men do, horses would paint the forms of the gods like horses, and oxen like oxen, and make their bodies in the image of their several kinds.

Fragment 16

The Ethiopians make their gods black and snub-nosed;
the Thracians say theirs have blue eyes and red hair.

Fragment 18

The gods have not revealed all things to men from the beginning, but by seeking they find in time what is better.

Fragment 23

One god, the greatest among gods and men, neither in form like unto mortals nor in thought . . . .

Fragment 24

He sees all over, thinks all over, and hears all over.

Fragment 25

But without toil he swayeth all things by the thought of his mind.

Fragment 26

And he abideth ever in the selfsame place, moving not at all; nor doth it befit him to go about now hither now thither.

Fragment 27

All things come from the earth, and in earth all things end.

Fragment 28

This limit of the earth above is seen at our feet in contact with the air;[6] below it reaches down without a limit.

Fragment 29

All things are earth and water that come into being and grow.

Fragment 30

The sea is the source of water and the source of wind; for neither in the clouds (would there be any blasts of wind blowing forth) from within without the mighty sea, nor rivers' streams nor rain-water from the sky. The mighty sea is father of clouds and of winds and of rivers.[7]

Fragment 31

The sun swinging over[8] the earth and warming it . . . .

Fragment 32

She that they call Iris is a cloud likewise, purple, scarlet and green to behold.

Fragment 33

For we all are born of earth and water.

Fragment 34

There never was nor will be a man who has certain knowledge about the gods and about all the things I speak of. Even if he should chance to say the complete truth, yet he himself knows not that it is so. But all may have their fancy.[9]

Fragment 35

Let these be taken as fancies[10] something like the truth.

Fragment 36

All of them[11] that are visible for mortals to behold.

Fragment 37

And in some caves water drips . . . .

Fragment 38

If god had not made brown honey, men would think figs far sweeter than they do.

Notes

Jump up ↑ So I understand ἀμφ' ἀρετῆς. The τόνος is "strength of lungs." The next verses are directed against Hesiod and Alkaios (Diels).

Jump up ↑ At this date "art" is the natural translation of σοφίη in such a writer as Xenophanes.

Jump up ↑ Diels suggests that this is an attack on a poet like Simonides, whose greed was proverbial.

Jump up ↑ The name of Pythagoras does not occur in the lines that have been preserved; but the source of Diogenes viii. 36 must have had the complete elegy before him; for he said the verses occurred ἐν ἐλεγείᾳ, ἧς ἀρχὴ Νῦν αὖτ' ἄλλον ἔπειμι λόγον κτλ.

Jump up ↑ Bergk (Litteraturgesch. ii. p. 418, n. 23) took φροντὶς here to mean the literary work of Xenophanes, but it is surely an anachronism to suppose that at this date it could be used like the Latin cura.

Jump up ↑ Reading ἠέρι for καὶ ῥεῖ with Diels.

Jump up ↑ This fragment has been recovered from the Geneva scholia on Homer (see Arch. iv. p. 652). The words in brackets are added by Diels.

Jump up ↑ The word is ὑπεριέμενος. This is quoted from the Allegories as an explanation of the name Hyperion, and doubtless Xenophanes so meant it.

Jump up ↑ It is more natural to take πᾶσι as masculine than as neuter, and ἐπὶ πᾶσι can mean "in the power of all."

Jump up ↑ Reading δεδοξάσθω with Wilamowitz.

Jump up ↑ As Diels suggests, this probably refers to the stars, which Xenophanes held to be clouds.

Note from the Editor

Odin's Library Classics strives to bring you unedited and unabridged works of classical literature. As such, this is the complete and unabridged version of the original English text unless noted. In some instances, obvious typographical errors have been corrected. This is done to preserve the original text as much as possible. The English language has evolved since the writing and some of the words appear in their original form, or at least the most commonly used form at the time. This is done to protect the original intent of the author. If at any time you are unsure of the meaning of a word, please do your research on the etymology of that word. It is important to preserve the history of the English language.

Taylor Anderson

Printed in Great Britain
by Amazon